SECRET CITY

poems

ALSO BY KATHERINE SMITH

Woman Alone on the Mountain
Argument by Design

SECRET CITY

poems

KATHERINE SMITH

MADVILLE PUBLISHING

LAKE DALLAS, TEXAS

FIRST EDITION

Requests for permission to reprint or reuse material
from this work should be sent to:

Permissions
Madville Publishing
PO Box 358
Lake Dallas, TX 75065

Cover Design: Jacqueline Davis
Cover Art: Kathryn Smith

ISBN: 978-1-948692-90-8 paperback
ISBN: 978-1-948692-91-5 ebook
Library of Congress Control Number: 2022932003

For Carla Witcher

TABLE OF CONTENTS

1   Heart Monitor

I

5   Shepherd
6   Nebraska Avenue
7   Forever
9   Red Shoe
10   I Drive Home at Dusk in February
11   Teach Me to Say Goodbye
12   Church-Going
13   Preserves
14   Mimosa
15   Easter Basket
16   Vultures
17   Ceremony, Late August
18   Pieta

II

21   Sukkot
23   Secret City
25   Rock of Ages
26   Mobile
27   Ghosts
28   The Reader
29   Camellia Japonica
30   Night-Blooming Cereus
31   Firepit
33   War Effort
34   Isotope
35   Lost Town

36	Spectacle
37	Chrysanthemum
39	Child
40	Cumberland Plateau Prayer
41	Dove

III

45	Tangle
46	Night Watch
47	The Mathematician Shaves
48	Gift
49	North
50	Cross Creek Road
51	Knicknack
53	The Wind Is Six
54	Buick Regal
56	Wildflower Guide
58	Zikkurat
60	The Bowl

IV

63	The Memorial
64	The Lawn
65	Blight
67	The Gates
68	Easter
69	Boots
70	World of Love
71	Omelet
73	Happiness
74	Smoke
75	The Farrier
76	The Bee

77 Horse God

78 Sunset

80 Forget-Me-Not

81 I Lie in My Hospital Bed and Throw Up

82 Beau

83 Worth Believing

84 She Shops for New Clothes

86 We Love Those Among Whom We Have Spent the Day

87 Real ID

88 The Real Journey

89 For My Grandmothers

90 Acknowledgments

91 About the Author

HEART MONITOR

Red leaves on the pin oak tree flip
from their dull brown backs,
toss and turn in the breeze, catching light
and movement.

Nothing is easier than to walk straight past the trees
like the minor poem of a minor poet,
easy to ignore, then suddenly visible,
shimmering, miraculous,
before the attention like so much wind
wanders from the light struck

and goes back
to where it was, an emptiness ordinary as ink
or a row of trees in your neighborhood.
So too you have seen the ordinary oak
of your own heart. Its aorta branches
from the ventricle beats
on the screen. No ordinary thing,

the way those thin branches jut
across the lawn of your childhood
home, bow toward the dead
grass, lift silver twigs
like an offering, and scatter
their spinning husks.

I

SHEPHERD

The neighborhood shines before dark
like a child whose parents have properly taught her
the limits of the world, the small beauty

of whirring air conditioners, newspapers
carefully gathered from driveways Sunday mornings,
then refolded at dusk, the last sun on the white

blankets of the Appaloosas grazing in the field.
You hope you have taught your daughter enough
about the temperature of grilled meat, about evenings

too cool for bare skin, about what one human
can be for another. Once you two lived
the only Jews for fifty miles

in a small town in Tennessee.
You hope you taught her well enough
how to read the book of the world

and not be haunted by its strangeness.
The swing-set has almost vanished.
On your evening walk, you dream that the night

about to fall on the neighborhood
has tangled in your daughter's hair.
You wake to a sharp bark from the white muzzle

of the shepherd that, young, used to rush toward you,
teeth snapping. Now her grizzled tail glints, wagging,
as she herds you back to the friendly road.

NEBRASKA AVENUE

Loneliness is turning up Nebraska Avenue,
in June, the street filling with people.
A young man with full cheeks and black curls
jogs next to a lanky older man she's sure is the father.

Their elbows touch as they jog easily up the street
that is a green negative space between them.
A mother swings a little girl in a frothy pink dress
to a stone wall and takes her picture

before plunking her back into a stroller
and vanishing. She's certain she will never know
any lover's flesh better than she knows
the pavement beneath her sneakers.

A white Pyrenees slobbers in the heat
behind a chain link fence. It's almost a song
the way the dog barks rhythmically at her as she passes.
She remembers the gray shepherd she had as a child,

her sisters and brothers, her loud parents,
all of them crammed into a small ranch house.
She thinks of the successes that brought her
to Nebraska Avenue, the good full-time job,

the semester over, the daughter in graduate school in Boston.
The man she'd left who hated her to drink coffee or think.
It is almost summer. A teenage girl on a skateboard flies past,
her black braids filling green space, her body

blinding, her music blaring, *I am the world.*

FOREVER

Young women stood sentry,
one at each corner
of the chain link fence.
We adored them
in their blue skirts,
white blouses,
our blond priestesses
presiding
over morning:
beneath blue infinity,
we hung upside down,
let our hair fall,
brush the ground,
passed a glass jar
round a circle until cream
curdled to butter. We
spun sugar to candy,
mortared gingersnaps
to roofs. As the sun rose higher
they moved among us
placing graham crackers
in our palms, pouring milk
into paper cups
by our crossed feet.
For a part of each day
they loved me,
one more child
in Tennessee
who wasn't going to hell,
which I was going to
definitely and forever
according to my friends
and their fathers.

I'd already decided
I didn't believe in hell.
But I definitely believed
in forever, which crept inside
the blue mats stacked
against the wall,
inside the blue-eyed teacher's
whispered, *Shush, shush*
as I lay wide awake at nap time
pretending to sleep
on the floor under my blanket.

RED SHOE

When Rick Dillon who'd insulted
my breasts all of seventh grade
told my sister her hair was made of wire,
I pulled off my red and white oxford
and told him if he didn't shut up, I'd hit him
and when he didn't, I did: slammed
my shoe across his nose. On the way off the bus,
I glanced back just once. Everything I need
to know about contempt, I learned from his face,
how when someone named Richard calls you a name
and snaps your bra, you don't just sit there and wait.
How when a boy spray paints a swastika on the street
in front of your house, you whip the kid who did it.
How everyone feels contempt for something.
Whether it's a girl whose breasts are too big,
or the Jew who lives down the street in your neighborhood,
everything strikes back. Forty years later I walk down
a pocked road running between two cow pastures.
The Tye River flows beneath a mountain on one side,
Taylor's Store Loop on the other. Just ahead of me
the path marked by flags where a pipeline will cut
through the heart of the Shenandoah. There are people
willing to let go of this silence forever
to bring shale gas inland for twenty years.
Another proof that infinite love isn't possible.
The need for money is real as this mountain
and not contemptible. But greed is another thing,
a bully whose smirking face the Earth will step up to
with a crimson shoe, a curse, and a beating heart.

I DRIVE HOME AT DUSK IN FEBRUARY

The first time the fields died,
I was thirty, visiting my hometown
when my brother drove me
through the new houses in the bottomland
drained of its swamp, even the creek
where we used to stand the horses to cool their fetlocks
                    gone.
The first time a piece of land I loved was ruined,
I wept as if someone I were close to had died.
It seems silly now, childish, the way
a girl breaks down and cries at a single harsh word
or a boy weeps the first time he loses his heart forever.

The same children weep more quietly
through their recitation of the Kaddish
at their father's funeral
while the congregation stands with them
and the rain falls, pouring down
                    father by father.

TEACH ME TO SAY GOODBYE

No need for
the reason five wild turkeys
run ahead of you, looking for a break
in the board fence where they can dive
into wild wheat, huge yellow claws
clapping against the asphalt of a country road.

No need for hurt feelings when the first swallow
swoops across your peripheral vision,
the glint that is your life,
followed by the flock you believe for keeps.

One set of wings after another
sails through an ancient elm
that somehow survived the last century,
disappears beyond what's hidden
by the green branches' span.

It's not your place
to know why two horses trot toward you
ears pricked forward, then, manes and tails
streaming, fly to the far end of the pasture,
leave you standing near the fence line
with words in your mouth, an apple in your hand.

CHURCH-GOING

As a child, I never went inside
the crumbling brick and flaking clapboard
churches of the Tennessee Valley
whose preachers' furious sermons
I flipped through on television
when the neighborhood kids were at church.
Sundays after lunch, in their yards,
(they weren't allowed in mine)
they'd tell me I was going to hell,
impatiently as if asking me to play
a game whose rules they were explaining to an idiot.

Adult, the churches whose interiors I have visited are few,
mostly beautiful, ancient and special
churches with blue stained glass.
In Reims the emperors and saints
above the archway are cracked
as old bone, each relief chiseled high on its pedestal
by the hand of a believer. Mold and damp
float through the transept, water-green
as faith. Light refracts through blue windows
onto pews of stone or mahogany,
onto tables of burning votives. I scan
for clues the Madonna's crazed glass eyes,
the Magdalene's faded indigo blue.

PRESERVES

You don't even have to open your mouth
to call sugar to this world.
The berries tumble toward you, curious,
as large dark eyes.

You don't need to make the ironweed stalks
purple the meadow, the bramble
of storm clouds break open
over the valley, the summer bloom

into monarchs and milkweed. You can't
force the woman in the clapboard house
who's lived her whole life here
to call you—*Come here, Sugar*—from the road

       to sit in a rocking chair
on her porch, swatting away horseflies
while she tells you the long story
of blackberry picking on the hillside,
preserving fruit with her grandmother.

       Finally, your words
crystalize in late summer, say grace,
say faith, say courage, say love,
gathered overnight in the ditches, with
ironweed, blackberries, forget-me-not.

MIMOSA

I drive a day from Tennessee, where the pink canopy's
a bothersome weed, northward
where mimosa's bewildering, suddenly
the cherished centerpiece of lawns. All summer
              in the South
wild things ripened to nuisance: the deer
by the dozen wander fields of Queen Anne's lace
to gobble tender squash vine. The blackberry bramble
threads through the cornfields. Milkweed uproots tobacco.
Even armadillos spill onto the shoulders,
glittering like gum wrappers. The gifts clutter the road

like foil. Even courage, faith, grace, and love
overflow, sparks in old eyes on porches,
dropping like hickory nuts, shells crushed
by split hooves, meat held in claws, leftovers
              for sharp teeth.

EASTER BASKET

As a child she yearned for Easter
baskets full of lime-green fake paper grass,
eggs dyed pastel, milk chocolate rabbits.
She remembers a spring Sunday afternoon,
heads bowed around the table, the bible on the sideboard,
her friend's mother saying in one breath, *Pass the gravy, please*,
in the next *You're going to hell.*

She remembers the Cherokee reservation
in the Smokies where her parents spirited her
away from the neighbors begging her to go
to hear Billy Graham at Neyland Stadium.
She refused to join her sisters in the moon bounce. Later

the world spread its wide skirt, sparkling
white dresses and patent leather shoes
bought on credit from Kmart
that floated, angelic, to the Methodist church altar.

Once a preacher told her she was as good as dead
like the deer skeleton by the roadside,
heliotrope growing through its ribs, the hip bone
still blushing pink, maggots in the marrow.
Somehow, she's kept on breathing the smell of mud.
She's gone on loving spring in East Tennessee.

She doesn't want to be saved.
She wants cardinal and thrush song
to forgive the bluets on the lawn
to wind up to the second-floor porch
to flit through redbud and willow to the river.

VULTURES

She never wanted to know the domestic life
of vultures, the way their squawks punctuate
the rustle of pines as they squabble for a roost,

their feathers and droppings in the ditch,
the scavenger's unsteadiness as it tucks one leg bone under
the sphere of its puffed feathers

and with the other yellow claw
grasps the branch. She never wanted
to see them sleep

in the neighbor's pines
through firecrackers and buckshot,
cater-corner from her kitchen

window, hunched above her street,
fifteen pairs of wings, like it
or not. She wants

not to smell the stench of their roosting place
through the black scarf she pulls over her nose and mouth,
or to see how pitiful the vultures are

when the wind flicks them
easily, again and again,
from the branch into the gusting air,

and their helpless wings catch
the blazing winter dusk as they sail
across the blood-red fields.

CEREMONY, LATE AUGUST

Though it was like weeping at the happiness
of strangers at a wedding I'd crashed,
I teared up as the boy, a blue yarmulke
perched on his crewcut hair, struggled
through his Torah portion, his haf-torah.

Two sets of grandparents sang the blessings
when the scrolls were taken from the ark,
when the scrolls were dressed and put away. Afterwards,
back in my car, I remembered how enormity
and chaos had poured down on me all night
alone in my bed. I was turning
                               onto the shimmering

interstate onramp when the ordinary world
of late summer, its dying brown leaves,
       renewed ceremonies
whispered, *Haven't you had enough?*

I remembered how faithfully
the boy sang his blessings, how he'd clung
to crumpled paper his grandfather had helped him with,
       as he stumbled through
his speech on charity and justice.

PIETA

Even at four, I believed
in what I could see, prayed

to wind in the trees, howling
closer than God, more convincing

than the revival tent, better company
than memory. Wind washed gifts

from the trees, laid at my feet
hickory nuts, acorns, oak leaves,

the fragrance of white pine. Rain
pulsed through October's fallen body

like blood from a ripped artery.
The voluminous canopy of maple

disintegrated into earth. No ghost
saved me. From the ditch, a leaf

of red sumac flew, a cardinal's
wings risen from the valley's lap.

II

SUKKOT

Oak Ridge 1942

I belong to pine trees covered in popcorn and paper chains,
to "Silent Night" floating to the rafters of the white church

where I sit at the center with a doll on my knees,
to the long wait between winter solstice and spring equinox.

I live in a world where autumn doesn't exist,
where sycamore and river birch are drab as squirrels

or my mother in her house dress mopping the kitchen
when it rains outside and nothing shines.

October days the blue sky falls into the green water,
roots and leaves and sky seen twice,

like Mama pulling her watered blue silk
dress over her head, flushed. Her joy sparkling

in my father's gray eyes repeats itself
in the dressing room mirror.

Every April glitters with its eggs and lime grasses,
sparkling crosses on chains around the necks

of girls in pink dresses and the body hanging
from the picture in the books at Sunday School.

My first life happened once, like a red flash of dogwood
when the clouds uncover the sun, a bleat

of ram's horn, dull honeys, half-tones
of shimmering wheat, hanging pears and apples,

autumn squash. Sometimes I look in my mother's
eyes and squint. *We wanted a little one,*

she says, *too little to remember.* I remember
not like Jesus' name, which is the way

the river remembers the white oak and pine
on its surface, but the way a cloud remembers rain,

how I know God's face. It's not Mama's fault
I don't exist anymore than it's the sky's fault

if a cloud passes over the sun. One day
I'm going to walk out of the church on the hill,

find a lake and throw in bread. I'm going live twice,
once baptized in the Clinch River,

once with the wild geese that fly over Norris Dam
toward the Cumberland Plateau and never look down.

SECRET CITY

At dusk I climb to the top of Black Oak Ridge
to a little cabin where I read on the porch,

listen to the family of squirrels scampering
up and down the chimney, shooing the possum

that loves the persimmons as much as I do.
The ground is slick with skins I spit out,

blood red and sweet as sunset. Mama says
I need to be home helping her with dinner

but with all this ripe fruit I'm not hungry.
In only a day or two, the wild creatures

will lick the grass clean, leave nothing
but acorns, sweetgum pod, dried leaves. Then

it'll be winter and too cold to climb the hill,
on streets named after states, past the little houses

Daddy moved us here to help build.
The *war effort* he called it. *Keeping you safe*,

is what Mama told me. I'm American
in a hushed city full of quiet Americans

slipping off to their shifts at the factories,
children with bright hair that still dazzles me.

When I walk home I hear families in the hutments,
the privacy of silver, clinking glasses. A mother

23

pushes a little girl on a swing. Smoke rises,
loud whisper from the government factory.

I'm not quite sure how my life happened.
But it's beautiful up on the ridge. I like

how quiet the trees are, not to keep a secret
or to forget, but because quiet is all they are.

ROCK OF AGES

Oak Ridge 1942

Mama wishes I was too young to remember
the hymn we sang in the children's camp

at Doverport the day we learned Vienna
had fallen to the Germans. But I still have

the address of the house in Berlin
stitched to my tongue like my own name.

I sang it for months after, a psalm.
I hum, *Jesus loves me* to make Mother happy.

She says it's wrong to love the woods so much,
that one day I'll see things differently. I knelt

at the altar once and the congregation wept
and blessed me, *Praise Jesus*. After, Mama

looked at me gobbling fried chicken, stuffing
biscuits, one for the birds and one for me

in my pockets, and her lips grew thin,
knowing nothing had changed, that I wanted resurrections

of sweetgum, sycamore, elm, and beech.
Where the choir of frogs sings in purple leaves

at dusk, the color drains from the tree canopy
and the granite bluff on the opposite ridge.

A person belongs where she sees the face of God.
I follow the night's song stubborn as Ruth.

MOBILE

Oak Ridge 1942

At school I color rough paper with chalk: Jupiter, Mars,
Venus, a scale that makes Earth's tiny blue crayon

tremble in my hands. The rings of Saturn
flash, blinding as the news reel at the Saturday matinee,

a close-up of famished faces in the snow.
I hang the solar system over my bed at night.

Hung low, it brushes my face like a woman's touch,
fingers combing through my hair in the chill

waiting room before I boarded the train
from Berlin to the ferry in Hamburg,

her good-bye kiss, kindling long burned to ash
beneath the school day's close consuming fire.

GHOSTS

Miriam, Oak Ridge 1942

Mama told me once I can't belong
to the dead, and then she said, *Mary,*

get down on your knees and pray.
She thinks if I pray hard enough

I'll remember only Wednesday evening,
Daddy in the kitchen loosening his tie

Mama mixing catfish with breadcrumbs
her hands pink and the flesh getting under her wedding ring.

After dinner on Wednesdays we walk to church
through the neighborhood. The white pine

and magnolia lean on the hillside
and each house has its own enormous tree,

white oak, maple, sycamore. I always thought
when I wasn't so afraid of my own house

I'd wake up. But now I have a memory I dream
about in church. When all the grown-ups are listening

to Jesus, I hear shattering glass
and a voice that sounds like love

Go and take Miriam with you.
No one is paying me any mind

caught up in their own prayers
so I believe I once had another life,

belong to ghosts only I can see.

THE READER

Oak Ridge 1942

The wind blew me here with a question.
I look for answers in the weasel's jaw

locked onto a field mouse, in the vultures kittling overhead,
sizing me up for the life inside me, then sailing away to roost.

Home again, I sit beneath the raptors on the roof. Here's the life
you can choose from, my mother says, presenting America

like dinner at her table when, ungrateful, I slip away
to read another book, go for another walk. I imagine a life

of cooking turnips for dinner, watching the pats of butter melt
into the mashed vegetables, pouring milk for children,

reading only by lamplight when everyone's asleep.

CAMELLIA JAPONICA

Oak Ridge 1943

The camellias tolerate this zone from April
until at least October, maybe even till Christmas

if it doesn't snow and we cover the plants
from frost in November. More enduring

than the peonies' brief late spring wilting,
the camellia survives beside the Victory garden

where it isn't needed, neglected beside
the squash, pea vines, potatoes, lettuce.

The neighbors who hurry past our house scowl
until my mother wants to hide the flowers under burlap.

I beg her, shame-faced, to let live the ruffled pink silks,
the candy stripes, the crimson and cream satin,

full cups of stamens and pistils. Some say
flowers are a luxury. Maybe so.

But I pile our baskets with blooms,
some for us, some for the neighbors

who'll call me selfish, pretend they don't want them,
not while the factory in the valley reeks of smoke.

The couple who lost two sons
won't come to the door. It doesn't matter.

I abandon camellias on the stoop. I'll keep
one red heart, to remember peace,

a few white petals, in the long years of war.

NIGHT-BLOOMING CEREUS

Oak Ridge 1943

Some evenings when Daddy's working late
we sit in the vegetable garden, admire

the border of zinnias, dahlias, blue hydrangeas
darkening in alkaline earth Mama dug, mixing red clay

with peat. I never feel closer than when we inhale
the sweet scent of Mama's grief, her light touch

of homesickness for her own mother and father.
When she says, *It's different*, I knew she means

my own lumpy grief, means, *You have me.*
We watch the squash and lettuce fade

and wait for the night-blooming cereus,
its petals like elegant white-gloved fingers

unfurling next to the shadowy vegetables,
petals frothy in the dark, pretty enough to share.

FIREPIT

Oak Ridge 1944

In a circle, boys and girls baptized in safety's holy light,
flirt and reach twigs threaded with puffs

of charred marshmallow, dripping meat,
the girls' hair carefully tied back, the boys

like priests in chinos and plaid shirts.
Though I half-expect them to have vanished,

their faces still flicker and glow each time I look up
from oak's furnace. Inside embers' rooms of fire,

a woman on the Bergenstrasse scrubs
cobblestones beneath the gaze of a boy

no older than my brother; I lift a heavy curtain
in London, behind it, rubble where once

our neighbor's house stood; women's faces
glow against the curtains, tell

me to stand back, and then, not trusting words
to keep me safe, load me on a cargo plane

across the ocean, to mountains in Tennessee,
hidden city circled by fences, white oak. We

crumple old newspapers for the bonfire
at the Kiddie Club's teen night, wait patiently

for kindling to catch, then sit on benches
or on the leaf-covered ground in two rows.

I lean against the shoulder of a boy who teases
I flew across the world for his kiss. He nuzzles

my hair, my neck. The flame rises white hot, licking
memory, burning until I almost believe him.

WAR EFFORT

Oak Ridge 1944

I wander the woods choosing trees to pray for
when the loggers come with saws and axes

looking for firewood. The trees won't be
five-hundred-year old hemlocks nor magnolia

nor the oaks with their whispering canopies,
ancient trees with their bark thick as slabs

of granite, more trouble than the loggers want.
They want tulip poplar

with a trunk that two men can clasp with joined hands.
A poplar tree that keeps

two houses warm for more than one winter
takes fifteen minutes to fell, another hour to chop

into logs small enough to carry home in a pick-up truck.
I don't know what to want for this world

where a man with an axe in his hand
can throw himself at a tree hard enough

to bring it down in a single morning.
I'm just a girl. I've understood I can't help

but love the world and whatever made it.
If it were up to me, my prayers would keep

the poplars from falling. Daddy calls that
treason, tells me to stand out of the way.

ISOTOPE

August 14, 1945

Glistening in August heat, the teachers stand
on blacktop, where girls jump rope, or break up

the boys' squabbling on the ball field. Briefly caught
in a stable nucleus, I wobble between ringing school bells

and home. My father comes back early
from the factory, his face ash gray and lay

like the first fallen leaf stripped of green
on the brown sofa while my mother brought

him coffee and they whisper.
You do what you have to do. The same words

he used the one time he gave me a whipping
after I'd used the Lord's name in vain
and ran away from the dinner table

to ruin my dress in the dirt crawl space
under the porch. I understand

my dad does what he has to do,
the same way the Atlantic has to slap

the Carolina coast; the Smoky Mountains
reach into the Tennessee Valley;

the Cumberland Plateau shushes Oak Ridge;
our prayers for peace at the victory celebration

rest on enriched uranium, unstable isotopes.

LOST TOWN

Oak Ridge 1946

When I lose the trail looking
for the lost town below the dam,

I find my way thinking of the boys
who hunted squirrels with bb guns

in Oak Ridge during the war,
making sure they could solve a problem

without the distraction of sorrow
the same way I might choose a dress the night before

a dance when I wasn't too nervous. Sometimes
I ask to make dinner for the same reason,

to learn what to do next.
I don't know how to make a decision that doesn't

have hunger at the bottom of it:
meatloaf, squash, new potatoes, milk, and bread.

I come out on the path below the dam where fishermen cast
into the Clinch River, with graceful looping motions

that mimic the electric wires strung high on the mountain
down to the power station with its constant low hum.

Deer pass through and search my eyes for the hunger
for mercy or peace that stills my empty hands.

SPECTACLE

Oak Ridge 1945

All I know is near to hand as snow.
I reach for it from the porch,

the heavy flakes that fall into my palms
before I pull on my gloves, take my shovel

to clear the sidewalk. I pause before stepping
into the yard, not wanting to frighten the birds

fighting in the brown garden
where Mother hung the feeder

among the dead stalks of sunflowers,
black-eyed Susan, coneflowers.

The spectacle of want
takes place so close to the house

there's no need to ask—as we do about
the children in the newsreels,

begging for chocolate, medicine, cigarettes—
Why did they? Why do they?

Here, my family's silent,
knowing it's the snow

we saw fall flake by flake
that fills the branches of the Douglas fir tree,

that makes the cardinals fight the jays,
the chickadees hop unnoticed

beneath the clash of red and blue,
searching the crust for fallen bits of suet and seed.

CHRYSANTHEMUM

Oak Ridge 1952

The man I've come to love, like Mother's garden,
showers me with forgetfulness, the gift

of light. But when he kisses me at night
the sun still goes down. When he touches me

I cry out, and though he tries to make sense
of the way his caress makes me weep, I can see

I frighten him. He thinks he reminds me
of chance, of things uprooted, maimed.

Sorrow is like the woods, I tell him,
when wind has gusted for too many nights in a row

through the crimson and ochre trees on the bluff.
When the wind stops, the earth's a chaos

of wet leaves, acorns, broken branches,
and no fruit left, not even windfall.

All the species I learned so carefully in school
and from the long practice of naming what's

right at hand— black locust, sweetgum, chestnut,
hickory, tulip poplar—suddenly unrecognizable,

bones in the aftermath, the solid mass of green
lost. I tell him he is like the garden

after the storm has passed when I tally up
what's gone missing, the silver tea roses,

the last pale pink camellias—and what's still left
to harvest, sugar pumpkin, a few jewel-

bright chrysanthemums left to pick.

CHILD

Now the war's over I go back
to learning my spelling words,

each day's list of minerals—
amethyst, turquoise, quartz—

scattered across black velvet.
I tumble rules in my mind,

a collection of polished miniatures,
small possessions, prefixes and suffixes:

Elimination, evacuation, nation;
enrichment, bombardment, revolution.

The alphabet drips on my tongue like rain
from a downspout—

vowels truer than sermons
consonants more trustworthy than pledges—

unfurl from sentences, bolts of silk
for new dresses after years of damp wool.

I taste every word in the dictionary,
every spoonful of pudding,

lick the etched tines of silver, every syllable
a stitch in a quilt of sound,

then start again from the beginning.

CUMBERLAND PLATEAU PRAYER

The preacher can scream
all he wants, but if

I go to the altar
it's a fib to keep him

from hollering about love.
Praying won't do any good.

I made up my mind about God
before I could lace my shoes.

I've prayed for a heaven of pine trees,
of woodpecker tapping locust,

since I've been old enough to look out the window
at moonlight on the neighbor's roof.

DOVE

The objects in my room—forest-green
lamp, stone cherub on the mantel

granite wings pebbled with shadows—
cast anchor. No longer adrift in night

no need to cry out to a lover,
to name what refuses to step into

the unbreakable day—my father
bending to tie his shoelaces, his temper

forgiven—I recognize
the red pattern of bears and lions:

crisp curtains stitched by a friend
no longer alive. The dawn calls

to the dove-gray walls,
You're going nowhere,

one of light's more loveable lies.

III

TANGLE

Some days you brushed the tangles
from my hair, solved math problems
for the joy of it, cheered me on
in the bleachers at the edge
of the softball pitch. Other
days you paced the stairs
of the ranch house, cursing
God and my mother
in strange tongues, weeping,
falling silent, then leaving
for the hospital where
you made ceramic mugs
ash trays, returned, months later
eyes glazed with chemicals,
resumed being yourself,
went back to teaching
until the end. You left me
the South where you,
a New Yorker, were
a stranger, where now
you are buried
beneath a purple oak
with skeletal branches
shrouded in spider silk,
silver cocoons. I get very close
to each gray twig
where the burgeon
untangles from the tip.

NIGHT WATCH

I remember my father's face
at night, among the torn envelopes
holding electric bills, the mortgage,

the phone bill, the house insurance,
the health insurance, the credit cards,
the home equity line of credit—

and I think of the mortgage
Rembrandt never paid down,
the debts for oil and turpentine,

the hog bristle brushes he used
in those exuberant years before the crash,
to paint the great *Night Watch,*

brilliant soldiers looming from dark
ebony, the costly chiaroscuro
never paid for. I see the humbled face

of Rembrandt's last self-portraits,
my father's brow, furrowed
in the dining room's dim light.

THE MATHEMATICIAN SHAVES

Each morning my father believed
he had a face, his bristle brush
swirling the evidence of soap

across his jaw, a mask of foam.
His long fingers twirled the blade
up his neck to his earlobe. He

whom I never saw with a hint of stubble
leaned forward, his cotton shirt unbuttoned,
to examine his shaven skin

with his little faith in flesh.
Behind the blue-veined temples
a tumble of human equations pulsed,

a confusion that shaving neatly solved.

GIFT

I never knew my father
gave my mother the cello,
a burnished beauty

with a long, waxed bow
he bought her for their anniversary
because she loved to play Bach, because

when she played, she forgot
her five children, the ranch house
with the damp basement, the red station wagon,

that most nights she cooked Hamburger Helper
in an electric skillet, had more than once
swallowed enough barbiturates to kill her.

But my mother could still make divine
music, hold between her knees a bow,
that brought the dingy house alive

like prayer, Saturday afternoons
as my father lay on the bed listening
to beauty, its rare promise

so easily broken.

NORTH

I wanted a voice like a taproot sunk into a single place,
branches shading the grass, land of crosses and gospel.
I wanted to be the voice of Earth
that said I was going to hell, blessed me
with blue mountains. I drive in a rental car

toward Alcoa to pick up my daughter
from the airport for your funeral. The Smokies rise,
familiar dove-gray wings from the halo of clouds.
I once lived where the peaks shimmer
close as prayer that made it all the way

to a destination that speaks back
in beautiful twang. The people I live with now
don't know these mountains,
and the mountains don't know

      the people who roamed here
from every country on Earth.
I've spent my life yearning for
the scent of a place, the song of a people,
the voice of mountains
I turn my back on, driving north.

CROSS CREEK ROAD

This world born from a windblown branch bends
at the knuckle-bones—fingers reaching
for water they will never touch—
rooted in a small mountain, skirted in pine,

rising above the pocked mud of pasture,
vines loose on spindly persimmon trees.
Scotch pine still loaded with last year's cones
rises over the creek

where black-crested titmice
peep in emerald-green stalks of witch hazel,
and with my eyes shut, I hear winter
rustling through birch leaves, smell winter

in moss on the fence posts, see winter's broken
light zigzag across the river's green-gray current, gather
improbably at the fork of the Tye and the James,
shine on the horizon where the world ends.

KNICKNACK

A man who loved chess,
whom I never once saw smile or laugh
and whom certainly no squirrel ever amused

spread the newspaper across his kitchen table
open to the diagram of pawns, king, knights,
believing the pictures of the famous match

between Bobby Fischer and Boris Spassky
would teach me to play the game
he played with such elegance

with two cousins
who lacked my absentmindedness,
a possession for which he chastised

me, that serious man, my grandfather.
Scolding me for being American,
and incapable of foresight, he

lay out the chessboard
with the calculations of great players
for me to mimic.

To this memory, I'm sad to say,
I prefer the neighborhood children,
who ran out of their house to the bus

this morning crying, *Mommy, Mommy.*
I am not their mother
anymore than I own the squirrels.

What I own is the flutter in my belly
which I inherited from my grandfather
who arrived in America from

a city near Kossow now in Poland
where the entire Jewish population
was put in a ghetto in September 1939

and then made to dig its own grave.
What I own is the best decision ever made
for me. Two generations later

I finally forgive his face
its joylessness, its grim pallor.
Here I am in this beautiful quiet place

filled with squirrels and children
walking through this neighborhood
holding the privilege my grandfather passed on to me

fragile knickknack, ivory king, calculation
I carry everywhere I go, wrapped
in the soft tissue paper of my life.

THE WIND IS SIX

Wind sways back and forth, a girl
settling on the black rubber swing-set seat,
face open to the world. Her legs pump.
Her lungs fill with the scent of hydrangea.

Sweat bees sting the back of her knees.
She is six years old. Her front tooth is loose.
Honeysuckle flies into her like curiosity.
Now it is almost autumn

and the teacher with the placid brown eyes
is walking toward her holding out her hand.
The girl inhales her multiplication tables.
She will memorize the world

and turn it into numbers.
She will take hold of her teacher's hands the way
she grasps the two ropes of the swing.
She will leap out of the seat and land with a thud,

knocking out a tooth she will never find
though she searches and searches the grass.
She will find instead the gap.
She will touch night on the roof of her mouth

where her ancestors tremble forever on the cusp
of a future they'll never see: a child on the deck
of a ship docked off the shore of Galveston clasps
the future like a doll to take the place of what's missing,

the apple trees in Odessa she hasn't forgotten.
Her great-granddaughter rocks on her knees
before the hurricane that blew away
the tooth she mistook for a promise.

BUICK REGAL

Stillness taught it to love the ditch,
this car sprouted from the grass,
wheels sunk into ruts, warped
metal wrapped in green vines

green ghost of the perfect
body born from the assembly line
in Detroit fifty years ago, delivered
into the hands of a father,

then passed on to his teenage daughter
who drove it until part by part
the engine let go:
at first just minor repairs

her father could fix:
the brakes, the muffler.
While she sat on the brick wall
and watched

the afternoon pass,
her father in his stained jacket
lay under the car and softly cursed
the transmission, loosening

with a wrench.
Now he's been gone
for decades, the man
who cursed under the car,

then, dipped in oil and clay,
sat to her left
at the dining room table
eating hamburger.

She looks at the Buick Regal
in the ditch in a stranger's yard, her past
reclaimed by vines,
mimicking the antique

human shape of the day.

WILDFLOWER GUIDE

It seems corny now
how she slipped the flowers
between the pages
of the wildflower guide,
how it seemed urgent once
to know the subtle differences
between the rose-purple knapweed,
with its fringed bracts
taped just beside the darker
purple threads of ironweed; the edible
white water parsnip
taped beside its cousin,
the poisonous cowbane.
She stood in the field
with her book in hand
reaching for flowers,
examining the stems
that still stick to paper,
each blossom dried
beside its name: crowfoot,
periwinkle, milkwort.
For years after,
she knew everything
she needed from the new
guide's slick pages:
her baby blooming
in the white crib
her beloved, alive,
glowing in bed. For years
the guide unused, torn,
dusty on the shelf
has waited for fingertips
needing again to ruffle

through the wisdom,
the confusion and clarity
of the buckled pages.

ZIKKURAT

You are the sukkah pitched halfway
between Berkeley and Knoxville, the city of her birth
and the city she grew up in. You are Kay's Ice Cream,
the consonantal stop, a ladder climbing a twelve-foot-high sugar cone,

rising over a rickety roof where the girl
leaned her head back to see a giant's lips suck
an enormous drip from the hemispheric scoop.
You are the kangaroo in the Jardin des Plantes.

You are the clock, ubiquitous as water
in every language but English where you became a silent fossil,
a knight, a knot, a knee. You tick-tock above parks,
touchable as in doorknobs, stealthy as jackknives.

You are the ark of the open hand
the Israelites carried through the desert from Egypt.
The Greeks picked you up. The Celtics lost you.
English nicked you on the trek. You lie like my father

inside a closed casket. The men chant their kaddish.
Your terraces crawl to a heaven of kinfolk, a word my father never used.
He ran from Brooklyn, into a land of Scots-Irish strangers
and lived beneath pine trees at the edge of Norris Lake

where his children were woken once in the dark
by an earthquake that cracked the tectonic plate
that ran under their twin bed and shook them to the floor.
You are the nickname he gave his daughter

who found refuge from kidney stones in Shakespeare.
You are the fake fruit, the most boring drink in Amerika,
Kool-aid. You are the shank laid on a plate,
the color pink. You are her kindred spirit,

the letter that won't leave her alone.
You are the temple English trekked from,
sidekick who hitchhiked a ride at the Qwikstop
with a trucker pumping diesel into his tank,

drove across the Smokies and kept going.

THE BOWL

My parents were foolish,
my mother and father
filled to the brim
with suspicions, with angers.
They argued over
tart grapefruit, singed bagels.
At night their curses and thumps
shook the walls of the bedroom
I shared with my sister.
In that ranch house
all the children shivered like cold
cereal in a bowl of milk.
Meanwhile, squirrels chased one another
through the creamy thicket
and up the poplar,
loosening its blossoms.
When I was a child
I soaked in the world
from the end of the driveway
on my bike, where
grape hyacinth drifted
through golden forsythia
while, indoors, my parents
burned. Even now the spice
of flowers ghosts the air,
the purple whispering,
forgive, the yellow
whispering, *life*.

IV

THE MEMORIAL

The road devours the trees and the mountain, like fruit,
excretes the miracle of convenience. At the end of the trail

a memorial looks over the valley, where mountains
crash into a shoreline of silvery pastures shot through

with pink evening light, where factories ride the fog
like freighters on a becalmed estuary. Above, the marble

memorial gleams so white the war seems to have ended
just a year or two ago though the tarnished plaques

give the dates of two world wars. Nearby
some teenagers are drinking and having a picnic.

I didn't hike up the mountain to judge the happiness
of children watching the sunset on a wool blanket

laden with bread and beer. I came to breathe,
a necessity simpler and truer than faith, to feast

at the common table of trees and mountains.
I came to memorialize a tiny patch of earth elsewhere

whose pastures, ashes, birches, and persimmon trees
have no marble to sanctify or save,

no monument but the common one of breath.

THE LAWN

On this grass in 1984
I met my true love
in front of the bookstore

where men in camouflage
brandish torches and a few women too
in fluttering skirts, march

not far from the Rotunda.
They chant of the past
but these men aren't the past.

The past was 1984 when
we lay under the ginkgo
the man who loved

the Ivory Coast and I,
and music from Mali
played on the lawn now lit

by confused torches.
In the future
where the black-shirted men

leave their shadows
behind them in the grass,
lovers will hesitate

to lie under the ash tree.

BLIGHT

I was born for the same journey as the birds,
the poem about the poem, the pure lyric
of the ovenbird in the wood
calling for a mate to end its solitude
from the top of the American chestnut tree.
I learned to distinguish the American chestnut
from the oak chestnut by the serrated edge,
from the beech by the clasp at the hooked tip.
I learned to recognize my kind by its serrated song.

I step into the woods this morning,
chasing the ovenbird, stepping around a pile
of mating dung beetles. Pure lyric
was once mine. I woke this morning

to fungus on the radio: sixty Palestinians
shot at the border the day the embassy opened
in Jerusalem, the president's Indonesian resort
paid for by China, and the Russian oil company sold
to Quataris to pay off the president for lifting sanctions.

Pure lyric was once my everyday speech.
The ovenbird calls in the tree canopy
of hickory and oak.
All winter I taught writing
to teenagers from Honduras
now scheduled for deportation.

I'm part of a vast experiment
like the Lego experiment
in which people are given Legos
and told to build, then watch
as their creations are destroyed

while their despair is measured
and recorded for eternity.

The sweeps never happen
where I can see them.
One by one my students—
Transito, Luis, Fernanda—
dropped off at the border
with their English composition skills,
their aspirations and their associates degrees.

Now it's May and I'm mildly depressed.
Pure lyric hasn't been my style for twenty years.
The ovenbird calls deliriously from the top
of the American chestnut tree.

THE GATES

The gates of my grandmother's city in the Holocaust museum
are displayed behind a glass vitrine, its welded iron,
the tongue of a vanished world I don't dream in,

a universe buried in a mausoleum.
Signposts in the English of Ginsburg and Byron
explain the gates in the granite museum.

The preservation of iron can't revive
the Yiddish that burned like a face in the fire,
the tongue that haunts the world, a dream.

Sheltered behind the Blue Ridge's inviolate mists,
protected by oceans, and—years from the past—
the gates of a ghetto open now behind glass.

Outside, on the mall, a man says the strong are supreme,
says the refugee and the vulnerable can leave,
pass through the border where nobody dreams.

He curses in English. We understand what he means.
A crowd gathers around him, silently listening.
The gates of my grandmother's city in the Holocaust museum
speak the tongue of a country that exists only in dream.

EASTER

You decided the year you planted
petunias and marigold in terra cotta pots
behind the iron grillwork
that if the burden of earth wasn't
too much for the balcony
it wasn't too much for you
heavy with child. Many years later,

in the neighbors' yard, little girls
in peach-colored dresses search for eggs
from what they mistake for a clump
of daffodils, sprouted through the body of a dead squirrel.
The children scream, run to their parents.
But you are in late middle age, with no one to run to.

Your life is made of glitter, mica, fool's gold.
On Good Friday, the student from Togo wore a cardboard
sign around her neck that said, *Trust Jesus*
in sparkly letters. She asked, *What do you live for?*
You smiled, answered, *I live to teach you*
to write paragraphs with topic sentences and vivid detail.
I live to teach you to make sense. She chuckled,
forgetting for one blessed instant
to praise Jesus.

BOOTS

She bought these boots to sparkle,
sequined red leather, the glitter of footwear
to remind her of galloping Appaloosas,

of pinon, ash tree, snow four feet deep on the roof,
of rounding up cattle and whistling to the dogs by day,
of starlight and campfire by night.

This was a love almost Shakespearean,
a fire she saw in shoe leather. In truth
she wore the boots mainly to work

where for fifteen years they were so comfortable
she forgot about them most of the time
while she was supposed to teach grammar

but mostly listened when a boy told her about his father
who was deported, when a young mother of four
said she'd been evicted from her apartment.

She could have been barefoot. Still
the boots served a purpose, wrapping flesh,
as the agreement of subjects and verbs also served theirs.

Now boots and words sit in sunlight
near the window, glitter long gone,
only the slightest stain of red left in the leather.

WORLD OF LOVE

The streets named after songbirds—
Warbler Lane, Mockingbird Road, Bluebird Court—
have been taken over by crows.

With nothing else alive in sight
you observe the wit of black wings
gliding toward a snow-covered mailbox,

tail feathers lowered for take-off. Then you pause.
On your walk through the neighborhood,
rich in children and golden retrievers,

your down parka bright blue and red,
you stop to greet a woman, alone in her wool coat
with her old Yorkie on its leash.

At home the white cockatoo fluffs its feathers
and speaks without stopping in verse until you
come to think love has been a mistake.

You cover the cage with a shawl,
store it in the dark. Outdoors,
you can forget the beautiful white bird.

The crows size you up, their bright eyes
full of laughter. It's a relief when they glide
to telephone wire, not finding you wanting.

OMELET

I'm slicing an onion in half,
then in quarters, then eighths, slicing
until the whole globe falls apart,
and I slide it into the sizzling music
of olive oil that turns the stinging flesh
sweet. While I beat the eggs into foam,
pour yolks and whites into the frying pan,
I think about the phrase "get a life,"

which I heard one student say to another
while I was packing up textbooks,
zipping my coat. I always
wondered if getting a life meant
another party in feathers and sequins,
another baby, another husband, a new car
with a bumper sticker that says, *my kid's on the honor roll,*
more sex, running for public office.

I tried the phrase out on Trudy the other day,
saying, *I'm going back to my real life*
as I tore off a piece of the sourdough bread
she had just placed in front of me,
slathered it with butter, filled my mouth
while she looked up startled,
"What are you talking about?

This *is* your real life," she said
waving around the kitchen,
under the table to the dog
farting in his sleep,
then motioning up the stairs
to the room I loved so much

with the branches tapping the window,
and the stars in the skylight,
and the blue-and-white-striped chair
where I'd spent hundreds
of hours writing poems,
turning up the heat, listening
to the sizzle of bitter
turning sweet beneath the flame.

HAPPINESS

We walked into the school board building in the rain,
my father and I, the July before the eleventh year
of my schooling began. My father in
the tan jacket with the zipper he wore
for all bad weather, winter or summer

stood behind me. I begged
the school superintendent, a black man
in suit and tie with a polite frown
to let me take the city bus across town
to escape the high school where I was the Jewish girl

whose family didn't belong to the temple,
whose brother chanted *Hare Rama* in the library,
who never joined Young Life to pray around the flag pole
and scatter to spread the Good News after lunch,
who ate alone in shop class surrounded by the smell of burning metal.

I was bad news. *Let me go somewhere else.*
The superintendent smiled. My father's shoulders slumped.
*You're zoned for that high school. You'd have to prove
the new school has something your old school doesn't.*
I thought hard. *I'll join ROTC.* The two men laughed.

My father took off his jacket. The superintendent
signed the transfer. For the next two years I took the city bus
across town to a school where no one knew me. The day
I never had to go back to the world I'd always believed was true
was the first good day.

SMOKE

The purple iris draw the fragrant curtain
to summer's entrance: the heat of crumbling mortar
of brick, the scent of flesh behind the flowers.
A man in pastel shorts, my father stoops

over a heap of embers, rib-eye, smoke.
A blue merle collie flaps its feathered tail.
A boy, my older brother, gone these thirty years,
is speaking words that spiral into willows.

THE FARRIER

The smith moved around the horse,
took each hoof in turn,
yanked off the worn steel
centered the new metal, drove the nail
with a clean smack of hammer,
missing the quick,
                the nerve-filled frog.
While he clasped a fetlock
between his thighs, the hoof cradled on his knees,
I placed a palm on each side of the horse's jaw
hooked my thumbs in the halter, breathed
into the nostrils, touched
the white blaze with my lips, whispered
no harm would come as the sparks flew
from the smith's hands, his forearms
                covered with burns.

THE BEE

At the bottom of the hill near the gate
a single bee, big as a knuckle
dive-bombs, chases me down the road,
smacking my face, my neck, my arms,
not stinging, at least not yet,
but so angry I wonder how I wronged it.

I pause to catch my breath half a mile away
near the creek. The bee, still there,
doesn't notice how the other animals
flee: quail flushed from ironweed,
wings whirring in a whistling blur.

The whole meadow scrambles to escape
except the bee that keeps me company,
                  harasses me for miles.

HORSE GOD

All afternoon they stand helpless,
the nippy chestnut pony and bay mare,
under the sky. Lush tails
sweep from side to side
across haunches, reach as far
as salt-stained bellies, miss the delicate
skin of sweat-soaked necks

where horseflies land for blood,
plague them in the humid heat.
The two horses shake their forelocks
from blood-flecked eyes. They give up
grazing, defeated under clouds
that have rumbled and moved on
all week. Then, this afternoon

the sky finally breaks, pours through
their coats to lick the sting from skin.
They play beneath the lightning and thunder,
gallop into the shed, chase each other
to the fence, bucking and twisting
their delight with water.

They lie down on earth and stand for rain
to wash the dust from them. Again
and again, they race through the downpour.
If they believed, rainy weather's
what they'd have faith in,
what they'd pray for if horses did.

SUNSET

I would erase forever,
the heroes who broke my heart
the father who dragged me to the scale
shouting "No daughter of mine will be fat,"

Rousseau who abandoned his ten children
while writing about the education of children,
Voltaire who wrote *Candide*
who was racist

and no one and nothing will be left in my heart
except for a few women planting gardens
on Connecticut Avenue
still smelling of earth and exhaust fumes

and bread and the bookstore—
Oh, the books
by all the sinners
tremble with goodness and wisdom! In one

Basho walks past a motherless two-year-old
and writes a haiku of great compassion
about the child
he abandons on a river bank.

I drop my pen
to attend to the needs of children,
whispering *sorry*
to whatever I break,

and pick it up again to write
of the beauty of sunset,
pink light on the rumps
of Appaloosas

grazing in the pasture,
the beauty of the world
that lives on mercilessly
in my human heart.

FORGET-ME-NOT

There are so many reasons to be born
I've left behind
to wander this back-country road,
on one side, cows, dark pines;
on the other, wild turkeys, granite,
a sweetgum tree shading the creek.
               Already, maps
turn this ordinary pasture
into the next neighborhood,
turn love into nostalgia,
toppled easily as pawns
by the machine I know as well
               as the mind
I left idling at home
covered by sumac. I pull aside
the honeysuckle, the trumpet vine
the barbed wire to touch
the forget-me-not.

I LIE IN MY HOSPITAL BED
AND THROW UP

I don't remember the hummingbird moth
or the crows that settled in branches of the apple tree.
The nurses who adjust the cocktail in my IV,

who soothe my pain and nausea with a froth
of Zofran and Dilaudid, who bring beef broth
have filled my world with blood and vital signs.

Once I was one of the roaming things of Earth.
I lived up close to bejeweled roadsides
leaping at the scent of alert brown deer,

the clatter of sharp hooves, the waxy cere
of beaks of starling whirling inches from my eyes.
Once I was a fox, a squirrel, a swimming otter,

a hummingbird that fought for sugared water.

BEAU

I push your door open with my nose.
My tail wags the roses off the desk. Quick hands,
the thing of yours I envy most,
catch the vase before it crashes to the floor,
set the glass away from the edge,
rearrange the stems in water.

Who cares! I have a better idea than petals
I can't rip apart and roll in.
Let's leave the rattle of freight trains
that shake the carpets and quilts
and root for moles along the river bank.
Let's go for a walk up the mountain.

You who taught me to sit and to stay,
who know which species of oak
drop bitter, which sweet,
who fill your palms with fruit,
put acorns into your pockets
grind them into flour, for you
I've learned to see, though poorly.

Here on Priest Mountain, I lift
a quivering muzzle into the wind,
at the top of the ridge, piss
on scat of deer, of bobcat.
I believe what my nose tells me.
Follow me across those pine trees.
We'll find a bear. Let me teach you how.

WORTH BELIEVING

At the preserve between the freeway and gym,
an island of sunset, insect song, and rattling grass,
I walk at twilight after a swim.
Sumac more vivid than the cars that pass,
and memory of blue water over brim
the distant cloverleaf onramps, morass
beyond the thicket where the traffic's grim
and eighteen-wheelers roar beneath the underpass.

This enclave's a brushwork of complex strokes,
a master's sketch that survived a fire, this bleak
paradise of wildflowers, the moon a wisp of smoke.
The future doesn't concern us. Now's antique
trustworthiness, unequivocal, a deep-rooted oak
casts soothing shadows, dark critique.

SHE SHOPS FOR NEW CLOTHES

She gages the thread count of cotton
by her fingertips, is most at home checking labels
for silk content in thrift stores, wanders

Market Square on a Sunday before church lets out.
Fond of patterned fabric, she buys the pleated skirt
with its print of white doves, the gray blouse

edged in a strip of black velvet snaking its way
around the cuffs, through buttonholes, along the collar,
slithering between her breasts. She sifts excellence

from mediocrity, good from evil. Tired,
she peeks in the front door of the church
next to the Urban Outfitters to check out the sermon.

Seeing her, the preacher lowers his voice to a seductive hiss,
Come to the altar and be saved. Unimpressed,
she has heard these words too many times before,

this mother who can find no shelter, exiled from her children.
On the banks of the Tennessee and the Holston,
her daughters wear shame more easily than she

who itches beside them. Eve scatters with the pigeons
into the square, and the congregation who took her
for one of their own turns back to the altar. She wanders

downtown to the S&N train station in her pretty new clothes
to watch the freight pass by loaded
with lumps of glistening coal, shaking the earth

under her feet, getting soot on the leather laced sandals
never meant to bear up for the long journey
into exile. Like all else she's outworn—

the belief once flaunted grown threadbare,
tattered with age—she flings her old clothes
under the sparking wheels.

WE LOVE THOSE AMONG WHOM
WE HAVE SPENT THE DAY

At the Starbucks at twilight, a stranger,
young enough to be my son, leans over the counter
clicking on buttons, his cropped head inches
from my mouth while he enters Windows,
taps another button, pulls up the internet,
then praises the photo of my cat on the home page.

We love those among whom we have spent the day.
The almost Victorian light of November dusk
shines on living hands. The boy at the Starbucks
picks up his cardboard cup, gives me a thumbs up,
walks into the light-drenched parking lot and disappears.

I take my computer back to my table. I remember
the last time I saw you was summer. I brought
key lime milkshakes. We ate them with plastic spoons.
The porch was so terribly hot
I asked to go back inside though you loved
sitting in the sun. You laughed, *Whatever you want,*
darling. As if it were the most ordinary thing
we rose from the lawn chairs and went in.

REAL ID

I take a number and sit in a blue plastic chair,
for the wait I was promised
would steal less than twenty minutes
from this perfectly beautiful autumn afternoon.

When my turn comes, I crack a joke with the official-
looking man in a badge behind the counter.
He doesn't laugh. A girl feeds my documents
into the scanner. I ask what's in it for me.

The man says, "Ma'am now you can walk
into any federal building or airport." I don't laugh.
These documents that meant the difference
between life and death for the man who lies

face down in the water of the Rio Grande
his little girl tucked under his arm
are for me an afternoon's hassle at the MVA,
annoying papers to laugh at, to fling

into a drawer back at home and forget:
passport, Social Security card, mortgage statement.
Spoiled and lucky and just plain ordinary,
resentful of wasting an afternoon of my life

on this fool's errand, I long to go home,
a wish I believe I share with billions
of my fellows on this planet,
to shed all my clothes, take a deep breath.

THE REAL JOURNEY

All those years ago when I crossed the Atlantic
with two hundred dollars in my wallet
and a three-year old in my arms
were not the real journey. Nor the Monte Carlo
whose transmission slid onto the interstate
as I drove my daughter to daycare
nor the days I hitched a ride to work
to classrooms of students who laughed
at my attempts to teach grammar.
The daylight was no more the journey
than ocean or freighter.

The real journey happened at night,
at the desk with the reading lamp
and a pen in my hand next to the daybed
where my little daughter was sleeping.
The real journey happened in the dark
remembering Paris, the lost lovers.
The real journey wasn't sitting in the welfare office
applying for food stamps or combing the lice
from my daughter's hair, not crying
though I'd missed a day's pay.
The real journey was the yarn
weaving itself from body and mind
until it was no longer a secret.

FOR MY GRANDMOTHERS

Take away my sex, motherhood, nationality, religion,
what is left of me but the koi pond in the park,

the white and gold and red and black fish
floating beneath leaves in green water,

gently bumping heads; a group of schoolchildren
with magnifying glasses and paper bags

looking for goldenrod gall in the wildflower garden,
led by a gray-haired woman in support hose.

I emerge bloody at each moment
from the deeds of those strangers, my grandmothers,

Anna and Flora, dead years before my birth
who boarded ships to Ellis Island, Galveston.

In one of my worlds I am pond, fish, schoolchildren. In the other
I am American, teacher, woman, Jew. In both worlds

I am born not of those who stayed behind
but of those who sailed away.

ACKNOWLEDGMENTS

Thanks to these journals where the poems in this collection first appeared.

About Place: "Preserves"; *Appalachian Heritage*: "The Memorial"; *The Arlington Review*: "Easter"; "Happiness"; *Blue Stem*: "She Shops for New Clothes"; *Boulevard*: "Mimosa"; "Teach Me to Say Goodbye"; *The Chattahoochee Review*: "Heart Monitor"; *Chiron Review*: "For My Grandmothers"; *Connecticut River Review*: "Secret City"; "Firepit"; *Cumberland River Review*: "Night-Blooming Cereus"; "Camellia Japonica"; *Cincinnati Review*: "I Lie in My Hospital Bed and Throw Up"; *Hong Kong Review*: "I Drive Home at Dusk in February"; "The Real Journey"; *Louisiana Literature*: "Rock of Ages"; "Sukkot"; *New Verse News*: "Blight"; "The Lawn"; *The North American Review*: "Nebraska Avenue"; *101 Jewish Poems for the Third Millennium*: "Shepherd"; *Peacock Journal*: "Pieta"; "War Effort" (as "The Choice"); "Isotope"; "Lost Town"; "Cumberland Plateau Prayer"; *Presence*: "The Reader"; *Still: The Journal*: "Forever"; "Smoke"; "Church-Going"; "Red Shoe"; *The Southern Review*: "Vultures"; *Zone 3*: "World of Love."

My heartfelt thanks go to Sandy Spencer Coomer and the Rockvale Writers' Colony, Trudy Hale and The Porches, and Carmen Toussaint at the much-missed Rivendell. Many of these poems were written at these wonderful places. Thanks also for the support and beautiful editing of Linda Parsons. Grateful thanks as well to Nancy Naomi Carlson (with fond memories of Stanley Plumly's workshops) and Marjory Wentworth.

About the Author

KATHERINE SMITH's poetry publications include *Boulevard*, *North American Review*, *Cincinnati Review*, *Missouri Review*, *Ploughshares*, *The Southern Review*, and many other journals. Her first book, *Argument by Design* (Washington Writers' Publishing House), appeared in 2003. Her second book of poems, *Woman Alone on the Mountain* (Iris Press), appeared in 2014. A Tennessee native, she works at Montgomery College in Maryland.

CPSIA information can be obtained
at www.ICGtesting.com
Printed in the USA
BVHW052009191022
649760BV00002B/126